Namibia

Note: Amounts and activity descriptions are for Fiscal Year (FY) 2012 funds only. Activities undertaken with FY 2010 and 2011 funds are in most cases ongoing. For information on 2010 and 2011 activities, please visit www.state.gov/faststartfinance. The figures provided here do not necessarily reflect the sum total of climate-related financing provided by the U.S. Government to this country; please see the Executive Summary for information on the methodology used to develop these fact sheets. Funding amounts are rounded to the nearest hundred thousand; totals in summary tables might not equal the sum of projects below due to rounding. For those cases where multilateral funds are listed both in the country fact sheet and the global programs section, the U.S. contribution to that fund is only counted once toward total U.S. fast start finance.

Support through U.S. Government Programs

Bilateral Programs...$500,000

Regional Programs Benefiting a Number of Countries, Including Namibia

- $2 million to strengthen climate resilience through the Southern Africa Regional Environmental Program
- $1.7 million to expand clean energy production through the Africa Infrastructure Program
- $1.5 million to foster private investment in renewable energy in southern Africa
- $1.5 million to help southern African nations transition to cleaner electricity sources through the Southern Africa Trade Hub

Multilateral Funding Directly Benefiting Namibia, to Which the United States Contributes a Portion

- $5.2 million from the Global Environment Facility (GEF); the United States contributed $60 million to the GEF for climate change programming in 2012

Descriptions of 2012 U.S.-Supported Program Activities

Bilateral Programs

The U.S. Trade and Development Agency's (USTDA) funding of $500,000 is supporting a workshop and two reverse trade missions on U.S. solar technologies. This activity will familiarize key stakeholders from the Southern Africa markets with state-of-the-art U.S. technologies, equipment, and services, as well as policies, regulations, and financing mechanisms that can support the implementation of solar projects in Southern Africa. It will also foster the participation of U.S. companies in the implementation of solar projects in southern Africa.

Regional Programs Benefiting a Number of Countries, Including Namibia

The U.S. Agency for International Development (USAID) is investing nearly $2 million in the SouthernAfrica Regional Environmental Program (SAREP) to build capacity among a range of stakeholders to integrate climate information into policies and practices. These efforts will be conducted with the Southern Africa Development Community; the Permanent Okavango River Basin Water Commission; basin communities; and the governments of Angola, Botswana, and Namibia. Benefits will include better science and analysis for improved decision-making; improved regional and basin-level governance for natural resource management; and the implementation of adaptation strategies to help communities strengthen resilience to potential local impacts of climate change, including fires, droughts, and floods.

- USAID is investing $1.7 million in the Africa Infrastructure Program to provide technical assistance and advisory services to sub-Saharan African governments to increase the number of clean energy projects that are brought to financial closure and construction. USAID will also provide capacity building assistance to help governments plan and implement sector reforms and implement institutional, legal, commercial and regulatory changes that are necessary to attract private developers and lenders in the clean energy sector. Overall, these activities will help to reduce greenhouse gas emissions from energy in sub-Saharan Africa.

- USAID is providing $1.5 million for technical assistance and transactional advisory services to enhance the enabling environment for private sector investment in renewable energy in southern Africa. The program will facilitate structural reforms in the energy sector that will foster private investment in clean energy generation (including hydro, wind, solar, geothermal, and biomass) and transmission projects.

- USAID is investing $1.5 million in the Southern Africa Trade Hub to strengthen regional capacity for clean energy sector planning and cooperation. This project will improve the regional enabling environment for clean energy and partner with the National Association of Regulatory Utility Commissioners and U.S. Energy Association to provide capacity building assistance to South African electricity regulators and utility operators to transition to clean energy-based electricity sources.

Multilateral Activities to Which the United States Contributes a Portion

- The Global Environment Facility (GEF) is providing $4.5 million that will leverage an additional $22.5 million in co-financing for the Sustainable Management of Namibia's Forested Lands project. The project, implemented by the United Nations Development Program, will improve sustainable management of Namibia's forest ecosystems. *The United States contributed $60 million to the GEF for climate change programming in 2012.*

- The GEF is providing $700,000 to support climate change mitigation activities within the $5.8 million Namibian Coast Conservation and Management Project. The project, implemented by the World Bank, will address the pressures on natural resources from competing land uses in the coastal landscape.

Global Programs in Fiscal Year 2012

- $230 million for the Clean Technology Fund

- $60 million to the Global Environment Facility for climate change programming

- $37.5 million for the Forest Investment Program

- $37 million for the Montreal Protocol Fund, which supports a variety of capacity-building programs related to the phaseout of ozone-depleting substances.

- Up to $25 million to the Least Developed Countries Fund, with a focus on meeting those countries' most urgent adaptation needs

- $20.2 million to promote the development of climate-resilient crops as part of the Feed the Future Initiative

- $20 million to support global programs to reduce emissions from deforestation and forest degradation, including the Forest Carbon Partnership Facility

- $18.7 million for the Pilot Program for Climate Resilience

- $18.7 million for the Scaling-Up Renewable Energy Program

- $12.6 million for agricultural programs and water, sanitation and hygiene programs to reduce vulnerability to climate change

- $12 million for environmental and agricultural programs with climate benefits

- $12 million to implement the Tropical Forest Conservation Act

- $11.7 million for disaster preparedness assistance that delivers adaptation co-benefits

- $11.5 million for insurance to support renewable energy exports to developing countries

- $11.2 million for hydrometeorological disaster risk reduction that supports adaptation

- $10.9 million for the SERVIR Regional Visualization and Monitoring Program

- $10.3 million for the Global Methane Initiative

- $10.3 million for climate change integration pilot projects that will test new approaches to adaptation and mitigation in key development sectors

- Up to $10 million to increase the resilience of key development sectors through projects funded by the Special Climate Change Fund

- $8 million to support pilot projects that increase the resilience of vulnerable populations to climate change

- $8 million to support centrally funded activities related to Enhancing Capacity for Low Emission Development Strategies, in addition to the national programs cited in individual country sections

- $7.2 million to support innovative approaches to adaptation through the Climate Change Resilient Development program

- $7 million to expand the use of energy efficiency and renewable energy technologies through the Renewables, Efficiency, and Deployment Initiative (Climate REDI)

- $6.6 million to improve the monitoring and evaluation of USAID's global climate change programs.

- $5 million for the Famine Early Warning System Network to support climate change adaptation planning by identifying potential threats to food security

- $5 million for global research to help people that raise livestock better adapt to climate change impacts

- $5 million for the U.S.-Africa Clean Energy Finance initiative

- $4.4 million to increase food security and the ability of small farmers to adapt to climate change through the Feed the Future Initiative

- $3 million for forest and terrestrial carbon measurement and monitoring in selected countries in Africa, South America and South East Asia through SilvaCarbon

- $3 million for climate change public-private partnerships to advance development goals

- $3 million for the Partnership for Market Readiness

- $2.4 million to establish critical policy, regulatory, and investment preconditions for sustainable clean energy programs through the Regulatory and Investment Climate for Clean Energy initiative

- $2.3 million to increase agricultural productivity and value by supporting clean energy applications for farmers and agribusinesses in low-income countries through Powering Agriculture: An Energy Grand Challenge for Development

- $2.2 million to support field applications of clean energy around the world.

- $2 million to support the Low Emissions Development Strategies Global Partnership

- $2 million to expand the Partnership on Women's Entrepreneurship in Renewables to additional areas in Africa and/or India

- $1.5 million to support the development of new research on key issues related to climate change mitigation and adaptation through the Consultative Group for International Agriculture Research

- $1.4 million to extend USAID's Climate Change Training and Communication program

- $1.4 million to support the Rural Resilience Initiative, which is promoting both climate change adaptation and food security

- $1.2 million to provide climate science and information to decision makers in developing countries through Columbia University's International Research Institute for Climate and Society

- $1.2 million to improve the management and conservation of natural forests for climate change mitigation through the Forest Carbon, Markets, and Communities program

- $1.2 million to promote partnerships between cities to address local governance and service delivery issues linked to climate change vulnerability

- $1 million to help states and provinces from the United States, Brazil, Indonesia, Nigeria, Mexico, and Peru integrate strategies for Reducing Emissions from Deforestation and Forest Degradation and other forest carbon activities into climate change mitigation policy

- $1 million to implement the Greenhouse Gas Inventory Capacity Building Program for Developing Countries

- 21 other climate-related programs totaling $8.5 million

Descriptions of 2012 U.S.-Supported Global Program Activities

- The United States contributed $230 million in FY 2012 to the Clean Technology Fund (CTF), which helps to catalyze clean energy investments in developing countries with rapidly growing emissions by promoting energy efficiency in transport, industry and agriculture. The United States contributed $185 million to the CTF in FY 2011 and $300 million in FY 2010.

- The United States contributed $60 million to the Global Environment Facility (GEF) for climate change programming in FY 2012. The GEF is the largest funder of projects to improve the global environment, supporting capacity building and innovative, cost-effective investments whose design and environmental benefits can be replicated by others. The United States contributed $45 million to the GEF for climate change programming in FY 2011 and $44 million in FY 2010.

- The United States contributed $37.5 million in FY 2012 to the Forest Investment Program (FIP), which helps to address key drivers of deforestation and forest degradation. The United States contributed $30 million to the FIP in FY 2011 and $20 million in FY 2010.

- The U.S. Environmental Protection Agency (EPA) and the Department of State are providing a combined $37 million of funding for the Montreal Protocol Fund in 2012. The Fund supports a variety of capacity-building and institutional investment projects and programs related to the phase-out of ozone-depleting substances, including a focus on completing the phaseout of chlorofluorocarbons (CFCs) and preparatory work to begin planning and execution of efforts in developing countries for the phaseout of hydrochlorofluorocarbons (HCFCs) over the next few decades. Both CFCs and HCFCs are potent greenhouse gases that contribute to global climate change.

- The Department of State will provide a contribution of up to $25 million to the Least Developed Countries Fund (LDCF), a multilateral fund created under the United Nations Framework Convention on Climate Change (UNFCCC). The LDCF supports Least Developed Countries (LDCs) in adapting to the impacts of climate change, with a specific focus on addressing the most urgent and immediate adaptation needs. The sectors and activities in which the LDCF has been most actively engaged include agriculture and food security, water supply, coastal zone management, and public health. The United States contributed $25 million to the LDCF in FY 2011 and $30 million in FY 2010.

- As part of the Feed the Future Initiative, the U.S. Agency for International Development (USAID) is investing $20.2 million to promote the development of climate-resilient crops – crop varieties that can survive under conditions of drought, poor soil fertility and high salinity, and crops that require fewer resource inputs, such as water, energy, fertilizer, and labor. Many of the projects supported will be implemented by U.S. universities and the network of research centers that comprise the Consultative Group for International Agricultural Research (CGIAR). A significant share of this research is being undertaken by the private sector. CGIAR projects are involved in providing support for crop breeding of beans, cowpeas, and other dry grain pulses to improve adaptation to drought, high temperatures and low fertility, and developing rice varieties that are more salt-tolerant more drought-tolerant.

- The Department of State is investing $20 million to support global programs on reducing emissions from deforestation and forest degradation (REDD+), including the Forest Carbon Partnership Facility (FCPF), a multilateral climate change fund that helps developing countries design REDD+ strategies. The Department of State's investment will also help the FCPF to pilot payments for verified greenhouse gas emission reductions from REDD+ programs with the goal of providing incentives to reduce greenhouse gas emissions while protecting forests, conserving biodiversity, and enhancing the livelihoods of forest-dependent Indigenous Peoples and local communities. The funding may also support other global REDD+ initiatives and partnerships with complementary objectives.

- The United States contributed $18.7 million in FY 2012 to the Pilot Program for Climate Resilience (PPCR), which helps vulnerable communities adapt to changing environmental conditions including drought, flooding, cyclones and other climate-related hazards. The United States contributed $10 million to the PPCR in FY 2011 and $55 million in FY 2010.

- The United States contributed $18.7 million in FY 2012 to the Scaling-Up Renewable Energy Program (SREP), which helps the least developed countries expand energy access and security while stimulating economic growth. The United States contributed $10 million to SREP in FY 2011.

- USAID is providing $12.6 million for agricultural and water, sanitation, and hygiene programs to strengthen local capacities to prepare for disasters and reduce communities' vulnerability to climate change. These programs will educate communities on the potential consequences of climate change and improve local capacity to prepare for adverse impacts of climate-related hazards, such as extreme weather events, by increasing and improving access to water and sanitation. These programs will also improve irrigation and water harvesting technologies; enhance rangeland rehabilitation and soil conservation techniques; and implement new climate-smart agriculture and livelihood diversification activities that reduce household vulnerability to droughts.

- Through its environment and agricultural programs, the United States' Peace Corps is providing approximately $12 million in assistance to its host countries worldwide. Globally, environment and agriculture volunteers work on projects that encompass environmental education, environmental awareness, protected areas and wildlife, agroforestry and reforestation, waste management, natural resource management, and ecotourism.

- The U.S. Department of the Treasury is providing $12 million in FY 2012 to implement the Tropical Forest Conservation Act (TFCA), which provides funding for debt-for-nature swaps that contribute to the protection of forests and coral reefs in qualified developing countries.

- The Department of Defense is dedicating $11.7 million of Overseas Humanitarian, Disaster, and Civic Aid (OHDACA) funding to help build partner nation capacity for disaster preparedness. In doing so, these activities also deliver important climate adaptation co-benefits by helping partner nations better prepare for the effects of climate change.

- The Export-Import Bank of the United States authorized approximately $11.5 million for short-term, export credit insurance to cover the sales of various solar and wind energy exports from the U.S. to multiple buyers and end-users in developing countries around the world.

- USAID is providing $11.2 million in hydrometeorological disaster risk reduction activities that support climate change adaptation goals. These include building national and local capacity on early warning of climate-induced hazards; disseminating climate data and products to people at risk; and mitigating floods through watershed management and other natural and environmentally sensitive measures.

- USAID and the National Aeronautics and Space Administration (NASA) are investing a combined $10.9 million to expand the SERVIR Regional Visualization and Monitoring System, which integrates satellite data, ground-based observations, and forecasts to provide information about environmental changes and to improve responses to natural disasters. The SERVIR program provides geospatial information and tools to government counterparts and key non-governmental stakeholders to improve their capacity for decision-making related to climate change adaptation, land-based carbon sequestration, climate-resilient agriculture, natural resources management, and health. It supports the engagement of developing country institutions with the SERVIR network as well as the engagement of other suppliers of geospatial information such as the National Oceanic and Atmospheric Administration (NOAA) and U.S. Geological Survey. SERVIR already is working with regional organizations and individual country ministries in Central America, East Africa, and the Hindu Kush. Starting in 2012, the program began steps to launch a SERVIR hub in Southeast Asia region and support its operation for several years, adding to the global SERVIR network. The Southeast Asia region provides an excellent market for remote sensing, geospatial information and decision support services for both climate change adaptation and land-based carbon sequestration. USAID will also support the establishment of a new hub in another region yet to be determined.

- The U.S. Department of State and the U.S. Environmental Protection Agency (EPA) are providing $10.3 million for programs implemented by EPA in support of the Global Methane Initiative (GMI), formerly known as Methane to Markets. The GMI advances the cost-effective, near-term abatement, recovery and use as a clean energy source of methane from such sources as coal mines, leaking oil and gas infrastructure, landfills, agricultural waste and municipal wastewater treatment facilities. The Initiative supports work at more than 700 projects in countries around the world. In 2011, GMI activities reduced greenhouse gas emissions by 30 million metric tonnes of CO_2-equivalent per year (60 MMTCO2e/year). The Initiative builds international cooperation for methane mitigation among 41 partner governments, including all top 10 methane-emitting nations. Activities supported with this funding include pre-feasibility and feasibility studies at potential project sites, capacity-building through technology transfer and training, development of tools and resources, and support for the overall management of the GMI.

※ USAID is investing $10.3 million in several climate change integration pilot projects that will test new approaches to climate change adaptation and mitigation in key development sectors. Pilot projects ("pilots") will focus on integrating climate change into priority development sectors in USAID partner countries. The pilots will address specific development challenges related to climate change mitigation and adaptation in order to identify the most effective ways to support low emission, climate-resilient growth. Interim results will be used as Agency-wide teaching examples, accelerating the integration of climate change into programming across USAID and promoting the dissemination and adoption of best practices. Similar pilots underway with FY11 funds are measuring greenhouse gas emissions reduced from deep placement of fertilizer briquettes in rice paddies over the traditional broadcast method in Bangladesh; testing various combinations of measures, including index insurance, to help small holder farmers in the Dominican Republic adapt to changing weather and climate patterns; and bringing civil society and local government actors together in select Macedonian communities to address climate threats and opportunities for clean energy and energy efficiency.

※ The Department of State will provide a contribution of up to $10 million to the adaptation window of the Special Climate Change Fund (SCCF), a multilateral fund created under the UNFCCC. This contribution will support programs in developing countries that increase the climate resilience of key development sectors, such as agriculture and food security, water, coastal zone management, and public health. The SCCF is open to all vulnerable developing countries, including Small Island Developing States (SIDS) and glacier-dependent countries that are not LDCs. The United States contributed $10 million to the SCCF in FY 2011 and $20 million in FY 2010.

※ USAID is investing $8 million to support pilot adaptation projects that address climate change impacts at critical intersection points with humanitarian issues to increase the resilience of communities and country systems vulnerable to climate change impacts. The projects will work to strengthen local adaptation planning through community-based disaster risk reduction strategies; assess the connection between climate variability and change, disasters, food security, conflict, and instability, including applying adaptation strategies to reduce risks and build broader social and institutional resilience; build the capacity of partner country decision-makers to use hydro-meteorological data and information to improve flood and famine early warning systems to support country goals for climate adaptation; and, build capacity for civil society and local governments to make sound and inclusive adaptation decisions.

※ USAID is investing $8 million for centrally funded activities related to Enhancing Capacity for Low Emission Development Strategies (EC-LEDS), a whole-of-government program that supports developing countries' efforts to pursue low emission, climate-resilient economic development. The initiative is working with approximately 20 partner countries to build capacity related to low emission development strategies (LEDS). Activities include providing targeted technical assistance to assist partner governments' efforts to build robust greenhouse gas inventories, conducting economic and sector modeling and analysis; promoting stakeholder engagement;, and implementing sustainable forest and clean energy interventions. Partner U.S. agencies in EC-LEDS include the Department of State, EPA, U.S. Forest Service, Department of Energy (DOE) National Labs, and U.S. Department of

Agriculture. Going forward, the EC-LEDS program will support partner governments in turning LEDS into actionable and implementable projects and programs, such as through Nationally Appropriate Mitigation Actions (NAMAs). The EC-LEDS program may also provide support to help build partner countries' readiness to access markets and scale up climate change mitigation efforts. This programming is in addition to the country-level programs/amounts cited in individual country sections.

- USAID is investing $7.2 million in the Climate Change Resilient Development (CCRD) program to support applied research and knowledge exchange on the emerging challenges associated with glacial melt and its impacts on high mountain communities as well as a community of practice around climate services to advance the state of knowledge and the capacity of developing country partners. Other activities will further improve the planning, design, and implementation of adaptation programs and support innovative approaches in emerging areas of climate vulnerability and adaptation through stakeholder workshops and pilot projects to test and demonstrate the efficacy of adaptation tools and approaches in SIDS, LDCs, and glacier-dependent regions.

- The Department of State is spending $7 million to continue supporting the Renewables, Efficiency, and Deployment Initiative (Climate REDI), announced by U.S. Secretary of Energy Steven Chu in 2009 at the United Nations climate summit in Copenhagen. Climate REDI, implemented by the DOE, is a global program aimed at expanding the use of energy efficiency and renewable energy technologies. It has three components. The Super-Efficient Equipment and Appliances Deployment Program (SEAD) supports the acceleration of global energy efficiency gains for internationally traded equipment and appliances by pulling super-efficient appliances and equipment into the market through cooperation on incentives, procurement, awards and research and development (R&D) investments, and by bolstering national or regional minimum efficiency standards. The Clean Energy Solutions Center (CESC) is a web-based, knowledge-sharing platform that aims to aid governments with the design and adoption of policies and programs that support the deployment of low-carbon technologies. The Solar and Light Emitting Diode Energy Access Program (SLED) is developing a global quality assurance program for off-grid lighting products and small solar kits for rural electrification. SLED also is supporting the expansion of the Lighting Africa activities spearheaded by the World Bank Group to new regions, including India. At the Copenhagen conference, the United States announced its intent to contribute $35 million over five years to these programs.

- USAID is investing $6.6 million in FY 2012 to improve monitoring and evaluation (M&E) of its climate change programs. Objectives include establishment of new, rigorous performance monitoring indicators and performance management systems and analytics to support effective impact evaluation at a later date (e.g., control groups, collection of baseline data). This work promotes accountability and guides ongoing learning and identification of best practices. Specific activities include developing adaptation performance indicators or indices to better gauge adaptive capacity and producing measurement tools, including improved tools for accounting for greenhouse gas emissions reduced or sequestered. An ex-post comparative analysis of up to five existing REDD+ projects will analyze how changes in tenure arrangements and property rights impact climate, livelihoods, and participation within communities and households. Possible focal countries include Zambia, Indonesia, Nepal, and Mexico.

- USAID is investing $5 million in the Famine Early Warning System Network (FEWS NET) to support climate change adaptation planning by identifying potential threats to food security. The Network uses meteorological data for monthly food security updates, regular food security outlooks and alerts, and response planning efforts. The program will identify national priority zones and populations for adaptation activities in Africa and build national and regional capacities to conduct climate change assessments to better understand variability in seasonal climate patterns. The program will enhance monitoring and assessment activities to identify early meaningful drops in food and water security of communities that are most vulnerable to climate change. This funding is in addition to the funding reported on the individual "country pages" of this document.

- As part of the Feed the Future Initiative, USAID is investing $5 million to carry out global-level research on making livestock more climate resilient in order to help people that raise livestock better adapt to climate change impacts. For example, USAID will support research on the development, identification, and introduction of livestock that are disease resistant and heat tolerant, and capable of living on low-quality forages and feeds without experiencing a decrease in meat and milk production.

- The Department of State is providing $5 million for the recently launched U.S.-Africa Clean Energy Finance (U.S.-ACEF) initiative, which brings together different financing tools of the U.S. Government to unlock low-carbon energy investments across Africa. The initiative provides grant-based resources from the Department of State to cover project preparation costs for clean energy and energy efficiency. These projects are then aligned with direct project financing from the Overseas Private Investment Corporation (OPIC). This funding is in addition to $15 million provided for ACEF from 2011 funds. In total, the Department of State's support will unlock hundreds of millions of dollars through direct OPIC financing and private sector investment in African clean energy projects over a four-year period. By addressing up-front investment hurdles and providing long-term financing, the initiative allows private capital to flow toward clean energy projects in Africa.

- As part of the Feed the Future Initiative, USAID is providing $4.4 million to expand conservation agriculture production systems, sustainable agriculture, and improved natural resources management, in order to increase food security and the ability of small farmers to adapt to climate change. Many of the projects supported will be implemented by U.S. universities and CGIAR. The investment will support technological improvements (for example instruments to support minimum tillage and no-till seeding) and decision tools for crop nutrient management.

- The Department of State is providing $3 million to the World Bank for the Partnership for Market Readiness, which will support efforts in developing counties to prepare for and pilot market-based approaches to reducing greenhouse gas emissions, including the development of emissions trading programs; monitoring, reporting and verification systems; and greenhouse gas inventories and reporting rules. It will also support a platform for technical exchanges and peer-to-peer learning on market-based instruments in both developed and developing countries.

- USAID is investing $3 million through the U.S. Forest Service in SilvaCarbon, an interagency effort to demonstrate and compare forest and terrestrial carbon measurement and monitoring methodologies and build capacity of selected countries in Africa, South America and South East Asia to use these tools and technologies.

- USAID is investing $3 million in one or more climate change public-private partnerships with the goal of leveraging significant additional resources to advance development goals. Examples of this work include directing clean energy and sustainable landscapes resources toward partnerships with renewable electricity, clean fuels, energy efficiency, sustainable forestry, and sustainable supply chain business partners. Additionally, adaptation resources could be directed toward partnerships with water utilities, insurance or re-insurance companies, tourism industry, agricultural producers, and others to prepare for and respond to a changing climate.

- USAID is investing $2.4 million in the Regulatory and Investment Climate for Clean Energy initiative to establish critical policy, regulatory and investment preconditions for sustainable clean energy programs. As part of this effort, USAID supports exchanges between U.S. and developing country utility managers through the Energy Utility Partnership Program to share lessons learned in renewable energy deployment, energy efficiency, demand-side management and advanced metering technologies. USAID also helps to establish policy and regulatory frameworks that increase transparency, efficiency, and private sector participation in developing countries' energy sectors. These efforts improve the performance of utilities, enhancing sustainability and reducing dependence on government subsidies. USAID also works to help countries overcome barriers to the scale up of small scale renewable energy systems through the Microfinance for Clean Energy program, which works with microfinance institutions, energy service providers, and other private sector partners to promote innovative renewable energy financing.

- USAID is providing $2.3 million for Powering Agriculture: An Energy Grand Challenge for Development, a new program designed to increase agricultural productivity and value by supporting clean energy technologies with applications for farmers and agribusinesses in low-income countries. This program will be implemented worldwide, providing grants and technical assistance to organizations, businesses, financial intermediaries (including investment companies), and academic institutions that propose innovative, scalable approaches to boosting agricultural productivity and food security using clean energy. Partners in the Powering Agriculture program include the Government of Sweden, Duke Energy, the African Development Bank (AfDB), the U.S. Department of Agriculture (USDA), and OPIC. This program is leveraging more than $15 million from public and private sector donors.

- USAID is investing $2.2 million to support field applications of clean energy. Several coordinated activities, including Vocational Training and Education for Clean Energy, Increasing Adoption of Renewable Energy, and Increasing Energy Efficiency, will help developing countries build capacity for critical energy sector reforms; develop credible and robust systems for monitoring, reporting and verification of greenhouse gas emissions; and create indexing tools to address local barriers to the development and transfer of clean energy.

- The Department of State is investing $2 million in the Low Emission Development Strategies Global Partnership (LEDS GP). Through workshops and collaboration on a wide range of topics, the LEDS GP brings together more than 90 governments, multilateral institutions and non-governmental organizations (NGOs) to share knowledge and resources to advance the development and implementation of LEDS around the globe. The LEDS GP advances these objectives through: 1) peer-to-peer learning; 2) regional and country-level cooperation and donor coordination; and 3) targeted development and implementation of analytical tools and capacity building activities.

- The Department of State is providing $2 million to expand the Partnership on Women's Entrepreneurship in Renewables (wPOWER) to additional areas in Africa and/or India. The goal of wPOWER is to empower women through economic opportunities while also increasing access to and adoption of modern energy services, including devices such as solar lanterns and clean cookstoves. More specifically, wPOWER partners are coordinating efforts to: (1) build and strengthen networks of women clean technology entrepreneurs; (2) raise public awareness on the critical role of women in increasing energy access, promoting sustainable development, and driving green growth at the local level in the developing world; and (3) build the evidence base on the economic and environmental benefits of integrating women into the energy access value chain.

- USAID is investing $1.5 million through CGIAR to support the development of new research, information, and tools that are critical to understanding key issues related to climate change mitigation. The research will be carried out globally, in multiple tropical developing countries and in partnership with scientists, researchers, and natural resource managers from these countries. In particular, the research will provide improved information about measuring below-ground carbon and human-caused emissions in peat lands, mangroves, and other wetlands; new modeling and analysis of the drivers of deforestation, forest degradation, and the barriers to increased sequestration; and research on the impacts of interventions to promote farmer-managed natural regeneration of trees in Africa.

- USAID is investing $1.4 million to extend its Climate Change Training and Communication program to ensure staff, implementers and key counterparts are up to date on relevant climate change knowledge and practices, national and international negotiations and policy development, and technical data. Climate change content will also be integrated into other sectors' training (e.g., food security, health), building on experience to date with integrating climate change into natural resources management, water and sanitation, economic growth and other technical topics.

- USAID is providing $1.4 million to the World Food Program to support the Rural Resilience Initiative, which is promoting both climate change adaptation and food security by developing and testing comprehensive risk management solutions for vulnerable rural populations. The program is piloting an approach in Senegal to generate knowledge and lessons both to inform the USAID Senegal Mission's own food security and climate adaptation program and as part of a multiple-country research effort. The approach incorporates four complementary tools for farmers: insurance, savings, credit, and risk reduction measures, and includes a rigorous evaluation process to test the impact of these combined tools on vulnerability.

- USAID is investing $1.2 million in a partnership with Columbia University's International Research Institute for Climate and Society that will provide clear, tailored climate science and information to decision makers in developing countries to help them plan for climate-resilient development. The program partners conduct research and, provide training, data development, and sharing and technical guidance to support the development of regional and global climate services and platforms where developing countries decision makers can easily access data. Technical assistance is also being provided to develop index insurance mechanisms as an adaptation tool for vulnerable households, and to incorporate climate science into the design of index insurance mechanisms.

- USAID is providing $1.2 million to the Forest Carbon, Markets, and Communities (FCMC) program to provide technical support to partner country governments and NGOs to improve the management and conservation of natural forests. When successfully executed, the FCMC will help to mitigate climate change.

- USAID is investing $1.2 million in a City-to-City Partnership program that will help cities in developing countries sustainably adapt to the impacts of climate change. The program will promote partnerships and shared technical assistance between U.S. cities and cities in developing countries, and it will engage poor urban communities in identifying and addressing local governance and service delivery issues linked to climate change vulnerability.

- USAID is providing $1 million to the Governors' Climate and Forests Task Force (GCF), a unique subnational collaboration between 16 states and provinces from the United States, Brazil, Indonesia, Nigeria, Mexico, and Peru seeking to integrate REDD+ and other forest carbon activities into emerging climate change mitigation policies. The GCF will help to mobilize and advance financing for REDD+ activities on a pay-for-performance basis; provide recommendations for designing carbon markets so they include REDD+ activities; build capacity for REDD+ activities in subnational jurisdictions in tropical forest countries; and develop institutions and programs for linking subnational REDD+ activities with ongoing national and international efforts. Support will focus on integrating national, state, provincial, and project-level REDD+ activities and architectures.

- USAID is investing $1 million in centrally programmed funds to support the EPA in implementing the Greenhouse Gas Inventory Capacity Building Program for Developing Countries. This program will help developing countries build capacity to develop greenhouse gas inventories and meet commitments to prepare and submit National Climate Communications, including greenhouse gas inventories, to the UNFCCC. Training will be conducted regionally in Southeast Asia, East Africa, and Latin America, and will include work in multiple countries.

Summary of U.S. Fast Start Climate Finance

in Fiscal Years 2010-2012

In December 2009, President Obama and heads of state from around the world met in Copenhagen at the 15th Conference of the Parties to the United Nations Framework Convention on Climate Change (UNFCCC). The resulting Copenhagen Accord committed developed countries to collectively provide resources approaching $30 billion in the period 2010-2012 to support developing countries in their efforts to adapt to and mitigate climate change. This "fast start" finance commitment was carried forward in decisions of the 16th Conference of the Parties in Cancun in December 2010.

2012 marks the third and final year of the fast start finance period. This report reviews U.S. fast start finance provided in Fiscal Year (FY) 2012 and summarizes support provided across all three years of the commitment, covering FY 2010, 2011 and 2012.

In accordance with the fast start commitment made in Copenhagen, the United States has provided $7.5 billion during the three-year fast start finance period. Of this amount, $2.3 billion was provided in FY 2012. The three-year fast start finance total consists of more than $4.7 billion of Congressionally appropriated assistance and more than $2.7 billion from U.S. development finance and export credit agencies.

I. Highlights of U.S. Fast Start Finance 2010-2012

Since the beginning of the fast start finance period, the United States has substantially increased its support to developing countries to address climate change. In addition to providing a total of $7.5 billion of fast start finance, the United States has achieved significant progress in several areas:

- **A fourfold increase in annual appropriated climate assistance since 2009, with a ninefold increase in dedicated adaptation assistance.**

- **Increased support for clean energy financing in developing countries from the U.S. development finance institution, the Overseas Private Investment Corporation (OPIC).** OPIC has increased its clean energy financing from $8.9 million in 2008 to an average of $663.8 million annually over the period 2010-12. This support has leveraged an estimated total of $2.7 billion in additional private investment over the 2010-12 period[1].

- **Increased contributions to multilateral climate funds.** Over the fast start finance period, the U.S. has contributed $1.2 billion to multilateral climate change funds. In addition to providing $148.9 million to the Global Environment Facility (GEF) for climate change programming, and $914.5 million to the Climate Investment Funds (CIFs), the United States became a contributor for the first time to the Least Developed Countries Fund (LDCF) and the Special

---

[1] The United States does not count this leveraged amount as part of its fast start finance commitment.

Climate Change Fund (SCCF), providing up to $120 million over the period 2010-12 (the 2012 contribution is still to be determined).

- **Innovative programs launched to catalyze significant climate benefits,** including the U.S.-Africa Clean Energy Finance initiative (U.S.-ACEF); the Renewables, Efficiency, and Deployment Initiative (Climate REDI); and Enhancing Capacity for Low Emission Development Strategies (EC-LEDS). In addition, U.S. support helped foster international communities of practice to accelerate knowledge sharing across regions through efforts such as the Adaptation Partnership and the Low Emission Development Strategies Global Partnership. Details of these and many other programs are provided below and in the country fact sheets.

- **Clear, comprehensive, and transparent reporting of fast start finance information.**

II. U.S. Fast Start Finance Through Three Lenses

This section describes U.S. fast start financing in three ways: by **channel**, **thematic pillar**, and **geography.**

A. CHANNELS OF U.S. FAST START FINANCE

As described below, U.S. fast start finance is provided to developing countries through the following channels:

- Congressionally appropriated finance, which is delivered through both bilateral and multilateral channels;

- Development finance, delivered through OPIC; and

- Export credit finance, delivered through the U.S. Export-Import Bank (Ex-Im).

Table 1 – U.S. Fast Start Finance by Channel[2] (in US$ millions)

CHANNEL	2010	2011	2012	TOTAL
Congressionally Appropriated Assistance (channeled through USAID, State, Treasury, MCC, and other USG agencies)	1,583.8	1,878.5	1,255.2	4,717.5
Development Finance (channeled through OPIC)	155.0	1,114.8	721.6	1,991.4
Export Credit (channeled through Ex-Im)	253.0	194.7	301.2	748.9
TOTAL	1,991.8	3,188.0	2,278.0	7,457.8

[2] Included in these totals are 1) activities that were conceived and funded specifically to achieve climate-related objectives, and 2) activities that provide climate co-benefits (e.g., biodiversity and food security activities). In cases where only a fraction of a program's budget supports climate benefits, only that relevant fraction has been counted, not the entire program budget.

The United States provides its fast start finance support through a variety of different financial instruments. All Congressionally appropriated funds are grant-based, as is all U.S. support for adaptation. Development finance and export credit agencies provide support in the form of concessional loans, loan guarantees, and insurance.

Congressionally appropriated grant-based assistance

The United States provides Congressionally appropriated, climate change-dedicated grant-based assistance via the U.S. Global Climate Change Initiative (GCCI) – a whole-of-government effort to promote low emission, climate resilient economic growth around the world – as well as additional Congressionally appropriated grant-based assistance that delivers climate co-benefits. This assistance is delivered through both bilateral and multilateral channels.

Bilateral climate finance

Grant-based U.S. bilateral climate assistance is programmed directly through bilateral, regional, and global programs. These programs are principally supported by the U.S. Agency for International Development (USAID) but also through the U.S. Department of State, Millennium Challenge Corporation (MCC) and other U.S. Government agencies. Allocation decisions for each program are made by the administering U.S. Government agency. Assistance is targeted to help the most vulnerable countries adapt to climate change impacts and those countries with significant opportunities to mitigate their greenhouse gas (GHG) emissions. *Specific details on U.S. bilateral climate finance are provided in the country fact sheets.*

Multilateral climate finance

Multilateral climate change funds feature institutional structures governed jointly by developed and developing countries, and they play an important role in promoting a coordinated, global response to climate change. Multilateral assistance – channeled through the Department of Treasury and Department of State – leverages funding from other governments, development partners and the private sector to enable large-scale infrastructure investments with a range of tailored financial products across a wide range of countries. As with bilateral finance, U.S. contributions to multilateral climate funds are allocated to adaptation, clean energy, and sustainable landscape activities.

Over the period FY 2010-12, the United States is providing $1.2 billion through multilateral climate change funds including the Climate Investment Funds (which include the Clean Technology Fund, the Forest Investment Program, the Pilot Program for Climate Resilience, and the Scaling-Up Renewable Energy Program in Low Income Countries), the Global Environmental Facility, the Least Developed Countries Fund, the Special Climate Change Fund, and the Forest Carbon Partnership Facility. Support to these multilateral funds is detailed in the table below.

Table 2 – U.S. Fast Start Finance to Multilateral Climate Funds (in US$ millions)

MULTILATERAL FUND	2010	2011	2012	TOTAL
Clean Technology Fund	300.0	185.0	229.6	714.6
Forest Investment Program	20.0	30.0	37.5	87.5
Pilot Program for Climate Resilience	55.0	10.0	18.7	83.7
Scaling-Up Renewable Energy Program in Low Income Countries	0.0	10.0	18.7	28.7
Global Environment Facility	44.0	45.0	60.0	149.0
Least Developed Countries Fund	30.0	25.0	25.0[3]	80.0
Special Climate Change Fund	20.0	10.0	10.0[3]	40.0
Forest Carbon Partnership Facility	10.0	8.0	tbd	tbd

EXAMPLES OF U.S. FAST START FINANCE TO MULTILATERAL FUNDS

The United States has contributed $714.6 million during the fast start period to support the critical work of the **Clean Technology Fund (CTF)**. The CTF catalyzes clean energy investments in emerging economies with rapidly growing emissions by helping countries achieve access to renewable energy, green growth, and energy efficiency in transport, industry and agriculture. The CTF has already provided funding for 26 projects, including the installation of one gigawatt of concentrated solar power across the Middle East and North Africa, wind power in South Africa, sustainable transport in Colombia and energy efficiency in Ukraine. These projects are part of 13 Investment Plans totaling over $4.3 billion which are expected to attract over $36 billion in total planned investments. The Investment Plans are estimated to reduce or avoid 1.6 billion metric tonnes of carbon dioxide over time – the equivalent of Russia's annual emissions.

In FY 2010, the United States made its first contributions to the **Least Developed Countries Fund (LDCF)** and the **Special Climate Change Fund (SCCF)**, multilateral funds created under the United Nations Framework Convention on Climate Change. During FY 2010 through FY 2012, the United States has contributed $80 million to the LDCF and $40 million to the adaptation window of the SCCF [3]. U.S. support has increased the average funding available per country, enabling countries to integrate adaptation into larger development programs that address multiple sectors and are therefore anticipated to result in more substantial and long-lasting resilience to climate risks. Farmers

---

[3] Numbers are tentative at the time of printing.

---

now have access to a range of climate-resilient technologies, such as drought-resistant crops. More communities around the world are using early warning systems, reducing their risk to disasters from extreme events, such as storms and droughts.

The United States provides multilateral funding to support all three phases of REDD+ from readiness (Phase 1) through strategy implementation (Phase 2) to payment for results (Phase 3). The U.S. funds both the Readiness Fund of the **Forest Carbon Partnership Facility (FCPF)**, which supports 36 developing countries in preparing strategies and programs, as well as engaging stakeholders, to advance REDD+; and the **Forest Investment Program (FIP)**, which supports efforts to strengthen forest governance and institutional capacity, as well as measures to reduce drivers of deforestation outside the forest sector in eight countries. The U.S. also funds the **FCPF Carbon Fund** to pilot an international results-based system that will reward progress made in reducing deforestation and the associated emissions. Together the FCPF and FIP have contributed to advancing global knowledge and technical approaches to REDD+, as well as supporting the strategies and programs that will lead to increased forest protection, reduced GHG emissions, and the many other benefits provided by healthy, intact tropical forests.

During the fast start finance period, the United States has contributed $149 million to the **Global Environment Facility (GEF)** to support developing countries' efforts to develop and implement innovative programs in clean energy and sustainable landscapes. Since the start of GEF's Fifth Replenishment in FY 2011, the GEF has committed nearly $620 million of funding for projects promoting sustainable landscapes and clean energy. Estimated GHG emissions reductions from these committed projects have already surpassed the GEF's Fifth Replenishment target of reducing 500 million metric tonnes of CO_2.

Development finance and export credit finance

The Overseas Private Investment Corporation (OPIC) and the Export-Import Bank of the United States (Ex-Im) play a critical role by using public money to mobilize much larger sums of private investment directed at mitigation through loans, loan guarantees and insurance in developing countries. In FY 2012, OPIC and Ex-Im provided over $1 billion in investments, direct loans, loan guarantees, and insurance to support the deployment of clean energy technologies. Over the three-year fast start finance period, these agencies have provided over $2.7 billion in public finance support. Those numbers do not include private investment leveraged.

OPIC, in particular, has implemented a substantial increase in its clean energy financing activities over the fast start finance period. As the U.S. Government's development finance agency, OPIC contributes to U.S. development and foreign policy objectives while catalyzing private sector investment. During the fast start finance period, OPIC's clean energy investments are estimated to result in the creation of 853 megawatts of new renewable energy capacity in developing countries.

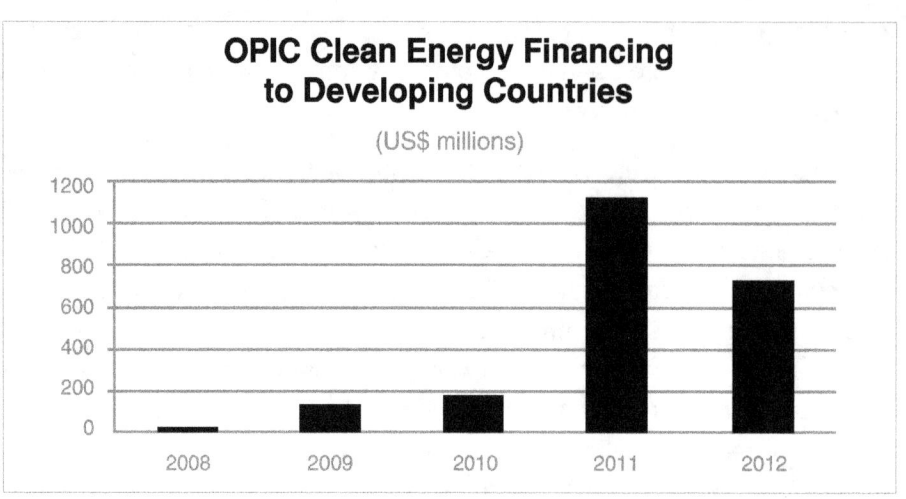

**OPIC Clean Energy Financing
to Developing Countries**

(US$ millions)

KEY U.S. FAST START FINANCE INITIATIVES OF GLOBAL OR REGIONAL SCOPE

At the recent Rio+20 Conference on Sustainable Development, U.S. Secretary of State Hillary Rodham Clinton announced the **U.S.-Africa Clean Energy Finance (U.S.-ACEF)** initiative, which brings together different financing tools of the U.S. Government to unlock low-carbon energy investments across Africa. The initiative is providing $20 million in grant-based resources from the Department of State to cover project preparation costs for clean energy and energy efficiency. These projects are then aligned with direct project financing from the OPIC. The initiative will unlock hundreds of millions of dollars through direct OPIC financing and private sector investment into Africa clean energy projects over a four-year period. By addressing up-front investment hurdles and providing long term financing, the initiative allows private capital to flow toward the most promising clean energy projects in Africa.

During the fast start finance period, the United States launched the **Enhancing Capacity for Low Emission Development Strategies (EC-LEDS) program**. EC-LEDS supports developing countries' efforts to pursue low-emission, climate-resilient economic development and growth. The program now has official partnerships with thirteen countries, with a goal of twenty partners by 2013. The EC-LEDS program supports the development and implementation of country driven LEDS by providing targeted technical assistance for efforts such as greenhouse gas inventories, economic and sector modeling and analysis, and forest and clean energy-related interventions. Going forward, the EC-LEDS program will support partner governments in implementing low emission development strategies through actionable projects and programs.

The U.S. has provided $28 million over the past three years to the **Global Methane Initiative (GMI)**. Formerly known as Methane to Markets, GMI advances the cost-effective, near-term abatement, recovery and use as a clean energy source of methane from such sources as coal mines, leaking oil and gas infrastructure, landfills, agricultural waste and municipal wastewater treatment facilities. U.S. assistance has supported technical, financial, or capacity-building efforts to more than 700 projects in GMI partner countries around the world. These efforts have led to actual GHG emission reductions of more than 86 million metric tonnes of carbon dioxide equivalent over the past three years.

During FY 2010 through FY 2012, USAID invested over $15 million in the **Africa Infrastructure Program (AIP)** to provide clean energy capacity building and transaction advisory assistance across sub-Saharan Africa. AIP is helping partner governments and agencies in African countries to plan and implement the key institutional, legal, commercial, and regulatory reforms that are needed to attract private investment in clean energy. AIP also provides specific technical assistance and advisory services to support governments in evaluating and negotiating clean energy projects.

Over the fast start period, USAID is providing $10 million for **Powering Agriculture: An Energy Grand Challenge for Development**, a program designed to increase agricultural productivity and value by supporting clean energy technologies with applications for farmers and agribusinesses in low-income countries. This program is providing grant funding and technical assistance to organizations, businesses, financial intermediaries, and academic institutions that propose innovative approaches to boosting agricultural productivity and food security using clean energy.

The Export–Import Bank of the United States has committed over $750 million to support renewable energy exports to developing countries over the period FY 2010 to FY 2012. These authorizations were made in the form of loans, financial guarantees and export credit insurance policies. This financing will result in the establishment of over 850 MW of clean electricity generation capacity mainly from new solar power plants and wind energy farms.

The U.S. Trade and Development Agency (USTDA) invested $59.6 million in 139 activities to support mitigation and adaptation in emerging economies between FY 2010-2012. Through the Agency's various programs, USTDA is supporting projects designed to advance the export of U.S.-manufactured clean energy technologies and services through funding for feasibility studies on clean energy infrastructure investments, technical assistance to advance the deployment of clean energy technologies and reverse trade missions for foreign public and private sector delegates seeking to purchase goods and services from U.S. firms.

B. U.S. FAST START FINANCE BY THEMATIC PILLAR

U.S. fast start finance falls under three thematic pillars: adaptation, clean energy, and sustainable landscapes, the last of which focuses largely on helping countries to slow, halt, and reverse deforestation and related GHG emissions (Reducing Emissions from Deforestation and Forest Degradation, or REDD+). The latter two pillars are often described jointly as "mitigation" because their ultimate goal is to mitigate GHG emissions.

For **adaptation**, dedicated U.S. climate assistance prioritizes countries, regions, and populations that are highly vulnerable to climate change impacts. By increasing resilience in key sectors such as food security, water, coastal management, and public health, U.S. programs help vulnerable countries prepare for and respond to increasing climate and weather-related risks. Assistance identifies and disseminates adaptive strategies; makes accessible the best available projected climate change impact and weather data to counterparts; and builds the capacity of partner governments and civil society partners to respond to climate change risks. Examples of U.S.-supported adaptation activities include, but are not limited, to:

- Strengthening government and local community planning, response and communications capacity for climate change-related disasters, such as floods

- Increasing water storage and water use efficiency and improving natural resource management to address increased variability in water supply

- Developing innovative financial risk management tools such as index insurance to help smallholder farmers and pastoralists manage risk associated with changing rainfall patterns and drought

- Distributing drought-resistant seeds or promoting management practices that increase farmers' ability to cope with reduced rainfall

EXAMPLES OF U.S. FAST START FINANCE ADAPTATION PROGRAMS

USAID is investing in the Glacier-dependent Countries Partnership to facilitate cooperation and expert exchange between **Peru and Nepal** on managing glacier-related adaptation risks, which are projected to worsen due to climate change. In Peru, the United States is working with community groups and municipal governments to restore and protect critical high-mountain grasslands that will help maintain a more sustainable water supply. At Nepal's Imja Lake, USAID is partnering with local scientific institutions to study the structure of the lake, working with communities to identify the risks that need to be managed, helping the national park develop a disaster management plan, and organizing exchanges with Peruvian scientists and engineers who can share what they have learned from managing similar risks in the Andes.

To help **Mozambique's** coastal cities become climate resilient, USAID is investing $4 million in 2012 in the Climate Change Urban Adaptation program to support activities that increase understanding of climate change impacts and strengthen municipal adaptive capacity and climate readiness. Activities include working with coastal cities to develop early warning systems and to strengthen planning and zoning in response to sea level rise and other climate change stresses.

For **clean energy,** dedicated U.S. climate assistance focuses on countries and sectors offering significant emission reduction potential over the long-term, as well as countries that offer the potential to demonstrate leadership in sustained, large-scale deployment of clean energy. The United States also supports regional energy programs that improve the enabling environments for regional energy grids to distribute clean energy, as well as global programs that focus chiefly on information sharing and building coalitions for action on net clean energy technologies and practices. U.S. fast start finance for clean energy goes to support the following activities:

- Promoting and deploying clean energy, including renewable energy technologies, energy efficient end-use technologies, and carbon accounting

- Supporting efforts to reduce gas flaring through the creation of domestic markets and productive uses for the otherwise-flared gas

- Supporting an improved enabling environment (law, regulations, policies) for integrating renewable energy into national grids

EXAMPLES OF U.S. FAST START FINANCE CLEAN ENERGY PROGRAMS

In **Colombia**, USAID invested a total of $17.8 million over the three-year fast start period to reduce greenhouse gas emissions through clean energy and REDD+ projects, as well as activities under the Enhancing Capacity for Low Emission Development Strategies (EC-LEDS) program. Since joining EC-LEDS, the Government of Colombia has begun to integrate climate change into its development objectives through its Low Carbon Development Strategy (LCDS). In addition to helping develop the LCDS, USAID support is enabling Colombian EC-LEDS consultants in seven government ministries to build sectoral climate action plans and create the Colombia National System for Climate Change. The EC-LEDS partnership with Colombia provides a clear example of how both the United States and its partner countries can benefit from technical collaboration to reduce greenhouse gas emissions while advancing economic growth.

OPIC is investing $16.7 million into Pakistan's first grid-connected independent biomass power project. The project will help **Pakistan** address its shortage of power, reduce its GHG emissions and reliance on fossil fuel, and ultimately serve as a replicable biomass model for the rest of the country. It involves construction of a 12-megawatt power plant in the Sindh Province, one that is able to exploit a variety of locally abundant agricultural waste products as fuel, such as bagasse, rice husks, cane trash, and cotton stalk.

For activities related to **land-use related mitigation (or "sustainable landscapes")**, including REDD+, dedicated U.S. climate change assistance works to combat unsustainable forest clearing, for example for agriculture and illegal logging, and helping ensure good governance at local and national levels in order to support the sustainable management of forests. U.S. support prioritizes mitigation potential; countries with the political will to implement large-scale efforts to reduce emissions from deforestation, forest degradation, and other land-use activities; and potential for investments in monitoring, reporting and verification of forest cover and GHG emission reductions. Examples of activities include:

- Supporting forest conservation projects that lead to reduced-impact logging, reduced deforestation, and thus CO_2 emissions reductions

- Supporting programs that help create incentives for communities to restore forested areas

- Promoting the adoption of: harmonized standards; methods to measure, monitor and verify forest-related emission reductions; best and transparent practices; environmental and social safeguards; and effective participation by local communities

EXAMPLES OF U.S. FAST START FINANCE SUSTAINABLE LANDSCAPES PROGRAMS

USAID has invested $12.8 million over the three-year fast start period in sustainable forest conservation and management in the Indonesia Forest and Climate Support (IFACS) program **Indonesia** is the world's third largest greenhouse gas emitter, home to a globally important tropical forest basin, highly vulnerable to climate change impacts, and an important regional leader and U.S. partner. IFACS assists the Government of Indonesia, communities, and the private sector to engage in sustainable economic development and to enhance food security, while reducing deforestation rates and greenhouse gas emissions in eight major forested landscapes covering 10 million hectares on Indonesia's three largest islands—Sumatera, Kalimantan and Papua.

The year 2012 marks the beginning of the third phase of USAID's landmark **Central Africa** Regional Program for the Environment (CARPE) with a $13.6 million investment. The third phase of CARPE will include two major components: the Central Africa Forest Ecosystems Conservation Project (CAFEC) and the Environmental Monitoring and Policy Support Project (EMAPS). CAFEC is a program that promotes responsible management of tropical forests. EMAPS is a program that strengthens central African nations' capacity to better govern their natural resources, develop new scientific methods to monitor changes to forests, and manage natural resources in a way that strengthens biodiversity and reduces landscape-related GHG emissions.

As an organizing framework for much of its climate change mitigation assistance, the U.S. supports a cross-cutting objective – building national capacity for **Low Emission Development Strategies**. The U.S. provides technical assistance to support partner countries and governments in their efforts to achieve long-term economic growth with a reduced GHG emissions trajectory.

The table below shows a breakdown of Congressionally appropriated fast start finance by pillar. All resources provided by the development finance and export credit agencies support mitigation activities but are not included in the table below.

Table 3 – U.S. Fast Start Grant-Based Assistance, Summary by Pillar (in US$ millions)

PILLAR	2010	2011	2012	TOTAL
Clean Energy	898.8	956.8	579.4	2,435.0
Sustainable Landscapes	249.0	361.5	276.2	886.7[4]
Adaptation	436.0	560.2	399.5	1,395.8

---

[4] As noted earlier, total 2010-2012 REDD+ assistance will likely be revised upwards as more data becomes available. In addition to the appropriated funds shown here, the U.S. also provided $900,000 in development finance to REDD+ in 2011.

FOCUS ON REDD+

As part of the United States' contribution towards Fast Start Financing, the U.S. announced in 2010 that it would dedicate $1 billion to help countries that put forward "ambitious REDD+ plans." The United States supports REDD+ activities as they offer cost-effective opportunities to reduce global greenhouse gas emissions while providing other sustainable development benefits. Since 2010, REDD+ assistance has been scaled up substantially to support the three U.S. objectives of REDD+ Architecture, REDD+ Readiness, and REDD+ Demonstration.

In 2010, the first year of U.S. REDD+ funding, we contributed $249 million to REDD+ activities around the world. In 2011, we significantly increased the scale and contributed $362 million to REDD+ activities. Our 2012 numbers on REDD+ currently stand at $276 million, and we expect these estimates will be revised upward as more data becomes available. Our 2013 funds are still being finalized; the United States expects to exceed $1 billion in REDD+ assistance in the very near future.

C. GEOGRAPHIC FOCUS OF U.S. FAST START FINANCE

U.S. fast start finance is notable for its geographic breadth – more than 120 countries received U.S. climate finance in the period 2010-12 across all regions.

U.S. clean energy programs prioritize today's major emerging economies and tomorrow's potentially large GHG emitters. U.S. sustainable landscapes programming focuses on globally important tropical forests, such as those in Central Africa, the Amazon, and Southeast Asia. The following chart shows the regional distribution of U.S. fast start finance only for programs that can be attributed to a particular country or region (the chart does not include global or multi-regional programs).

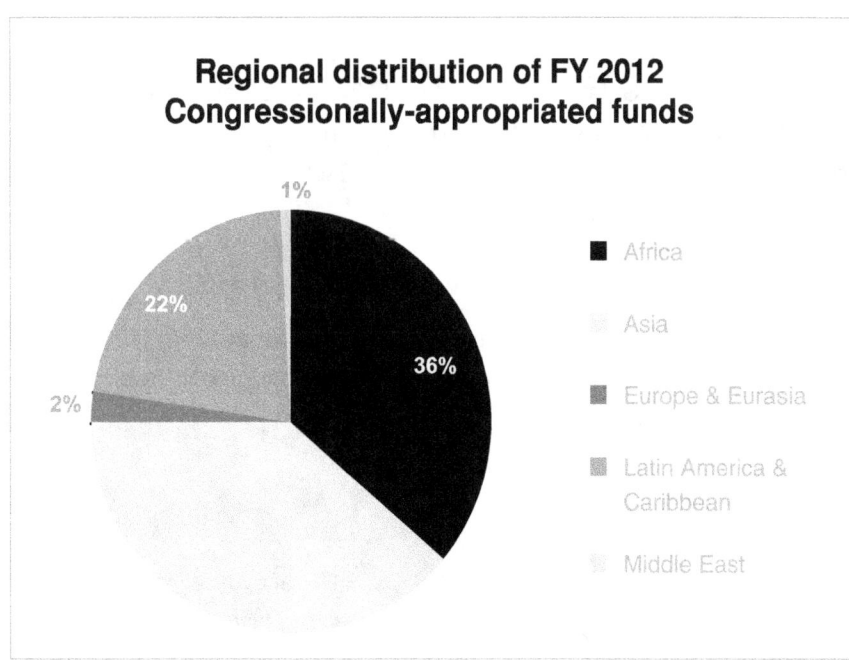

For adaptation assistance, the United States prioritizes its support to the most vulnerable developing countries, such as the Least Developed Countries (LDCs), Small Island Developing States (SIDS) and Africa, in line with the commitments made in the Copenhagen Accord. In FY 2012, the U.S. has provided nearly 80% of its country-specific adaptation funding to LDCs, SIDS or Africa[5].

III. Looking Ahead

Public finance will continue to play a critical role beyond the fast start period, particularly for adaptation. For this reason, the United States remains committed to providing public climate finance contributions in the years beyond 2012.

However, public finance alone will not be sufficient to address climate change. Our collective aim must be to combine a finite core of public money with targeted policies to substantially increase private flows into climate-friendly investments in both mitigation and adaptation. These resources will be especially important as developed countries, including the United States, work towards a collective goal of mobilizing $100 billion per year in climate change finance for developing countries by 2020, in the context of meaningful mitigation actions and transparency on implementation. The United States is laying the foundation for larger scale investments in the post fast start period by beginning to integrate climate change into its full portfolio of development assistance; by encouraging development finance and export credit agencies, such as OPIC and Ex-Im, to invest in clean energy technologies; and by leveraging significant private sector investments across all three pillars through multilateral programs. Meaningful mitigation actions and transparency in implementation will in turn serve an important role in enabling and spurring the mobilization of resources toward the 2020 goal.

IV. U.S. Fast Start Finance Country Fact Sheets

In addition to this summary, the U.S. fast start report for FY 2012 contains individual fact sheets, organized by region, for countries receiving U.S. fast start finance for *FY 2012 only* (for FY 2011 and FY 2010 fact sheets, see www.state.gov/faststartfinance). Each country fact sheet describes activities funded by the United States in FY 2012, including:

- U.S. Government bilateral programs focused exclusively in that country;
- U.S. Government regional programs that benefit that country among others (e.g., activities undertaken by the USAID Regional Development Mission for Asia);
- Projects financed by OPIC and Ex-Im; and

---

[5] Global and multi-regional programs – which also benefit LDCs, SIDS, and Africa in many cases – are not included when calculating this figure. These programs' benefits are spread across many countries, and cannot be narrowly attributed to any single country.

- Initiatives funded by multilateral climate funds to which the United States is a donor (e.g., programs undertaken by the FCPF).

In addition, almost $716 million of U.S. fast start finance in FY 2012 is being delivered through global and multi-regional programs whose benefits cannot be narrowly attributed to any single country.

While aiming to cover as many initiatives as possible, the fact sheets do not capture all activities, including procurement-sensitive activities or activities with ancillary climate change benefits.

In many instances, the FY 2012 finance reported for certain projects is only a portion of the ongoing funding associated with those projects, and projects undertaken with funding from any one fiscal year are typically carried out over multiple years. For example, implementation of activities undertaken with FY 2011 funds is, in most cases, still ongoing.

Fast start finance data for FY 2012 will continue to evolve as some projects are still being developed. Updated information will be provided as appropriate.

The data presented in this report represents a snapshot at the time of writing, and will continue to evolve as more information becomes available and as projects are further developed. The FY 2010 and FY 2011 totals reported here reflect slight revisions to previously reported levels, based on additional information received since the release of the 2011 report.

The fact sheets also include some programs with significant and measurable climate co-benefits (e.g., relevant biodiversity and food security activities). However, this update does not capture the totality of co-benefits provided through U.S. support.

For multilateral programs and projects, fact sheets differentiate between the total amount provided by the multilateral fund and the U.S. contribution to that fund in FY 2012. Only the U.S. FY 2012 contribution to the fund is included in the total U.S. FY 2012 fast start finance figures. In addition, this update does not discuss activities with climate co-benefits that fall under the regular programs of multilateral institutions, such as the World Bank, regional development banks, or United Nations agencies, such as the United Nations Development Program. However, as the United States is the largest contributor to many of these institutions, the additional climate benefits from such programs attributable to U.S. support are substantial.